KU-167-683

THE
NSPCC
BOOK OF
FAMOUS
FAUX PAS

THE
NSPCC
BOOK OF
FAMOUS
FAUX PAS

Embarrassing moments, Gaffes and Clangers

Edited by FIONA SNELSON

with a Foreword by
Her Royal Highness
THE PRINCESS MARGARET,
Countess of Snowdon

CENTURY

LONDON   SYDNEY   AUCKLAND   JOHANNESBURG

Copyright introduction © Fiona Snelson 1990

All rights reserved

Published in Great Britain in 1990 by Century
An imprint of Random Century Ltd
20 Vauxhall Bridge Road, London SW1V 2SA

Century Hutchinson Australia (Pty) Ltd
20 Alfred Street, Milsons Point,
Sydney, NSW 2061, Australia

Century Hutchinson New Zealand Ltd
PO Box 40-086, 32-34 View Road,
Glenfield, Auckland 10, New Zealand

Century Hutchinson South Africa (Pty) Ltd
PO Box 337, Bergvlei 2012, South Africa

Fiona Snelson's right to be identified as
the author of the introduction has been
asserted by her in accordance with the
Copyright, Designs and Patents Act, 1988.

Set in Times Roman by
SX Composing Ltd, Rayleigh, Essex

Printed and bound in Great Britain by
Mackays & Chatham, Chatham, Kent

*British Library Cataloguing in Publication data
NSPCC book of famous faux pas.
1. Humorous prose in English, 1945-. Special subjects:
Gaffes – Anthologies
I. Snelson, Fiona
828.9140208*

ISBN 0-7126-3635-8

CONTENTS

Introduction

Dining in style

A slip of the tongue

God given

Your Royal Highness

Trains and boats and planes

My lords, ladies and gentlemen

Hitting the right note

Accidents will happen

Personal appearance

What the eye doesn't see

A case of mistaken identity

A day in politics

The opposite sex

On the box

Never work with animals or children

Sporting gestures

INTRODUCTION

From my birth in 1968 until my final year at Norwich High School in 1986 I had a blissfully happy childhood, and it was during the final year at school that I became involved in the school social services and in particular raising funds for a local NSPCC appeal in Norwich. This was my first realization that not all children were so fortunate as I had been and that many thousands throughout the world suffer abuse, starvation, sickness and deprivation. When I left school at eighteen I wanted to continue to raise funds for children's charities but wasn't sure how. One evening I was at a restaurant with my parents and some friends and my father had just told one of his favourite stories about an incident which had happened when I was seven years old.

We were on holiday in America in February 1975, and were dining in a swanky restaurant. My father ordered a bottle of wine and when the wine arrived and the wine waiter had poured it, my father tasted the wine and politely complained that he did not think it was quite right. The wine waiter poured a little of the wine into a silver taster, swished it, sniffed it, sipped it, and eventually said, rather condescendingly, 'Sir is probably right.'

I must have sensed my father's embarrassment because I said, 'Excuse me, my daddy will be right because mummy bought him a book on wine for Christmas.' The wine waiter walked away with a knowing look to bring a new bottle of wine to this five-week wine expert. This apparently was my first 'faux-pas' which is regularly recounted at dinner parties.

It struck me then that everyone must have some story or experience that makes them squirm or chuckle when remembered and I thought it would be a good idea if I could get famous people to share some of these magic moments with the rest of us. The idea for a book of 'famous faux pas' was born.

I wrote over a thousand letters to well known personalities from the world of politics, sport, entertainment and religion asking them to recount any of these experiences which they remembered and finally this book was completed.

I would like to thank everyone who helped to make this idea into a reality, in particular my mother, who did most of the research, the NSPCC for all their help and encouragement and of course all the people who so generously took up their valuable time to reply to my letters.

I would also like to thank my mother and father for giving me the kind of childhood that I wish all children could have.

FIONA SNELSON, 1990

FOREWORD

KENSINGTON PALACE
W8 4PU

There is nothing more important than loving and caring for children. That is why we must listen to what they are saying or asking and why we must give the NSPCC all the support we can.

Some children have much to say and to contribute. Sometimes some people do not listen to them enough in order to learn how to understand them or to provide the love and care they need to grow up happily and in safety.

Still too many children go unheard, and live lives full of fear and pain caused by neglect and physical, sexual and emotional abuse.

The NSPCC, however, does listen to children and acts to help and protect thousands of them from all forms of cruelty every day. The NSPCC is always there – the children's friend who never says no to a cry for help and who will not rest until the child at risk is safe. Therefore I ask for your help for this Society's great work.

Margaret

President, National Society for the
Prevention of Cruelty to Children

DINING IN STYLE . . .

JEFFREY ARCHER

SIR HUGH CASSON

THE DUKE OF BEDFORD

PETER BOTTOMLEY

BARBARA CARTLAND

SAMMY CAHN

TONY HUSBAND

When I was 22/23 years old I worked as a personal assistant to Lord Harlech in his capacity of President of the European Movement and in this capacity I was invited to dinner with Nelson Rockefeller. The dinner was for ten people and I was by far the most junior and insignificant. On the wall behind Mr Rockefeller was a picture which I greatly admired and I felt confident I had seen it before. I did not speak during the meal until Mr Rockefeller noticed that I was staring at the picture behind him and he asked me if I liked the picture. 'Yes,' I replied, 'and I think I can tell you where the original hangs.'

There was a stunned silence around the table that was rescued by Mr Rockefeller saying, 'You are quite right, Goya painted two of that particular lady and the first one is in the Prado in Madrid.' It was the first moment in my life when I realized that a private person could own a Goya.

JEFFREY ARCHER

I remember a *faux pas* related to me by my dear friend, the late Sir Hugh Wheldon.

He had been invited to a party on a Thursday in September. He turned up, and rang the bell. His hostess answered it wearing a dressing gown and with her hair wrapped in a towel. She stared at him in icy disbelief.

'I am so sorry,' said Hugh. 'It must be *next* Thursday. Heavens forgive me!'

'It was last Thursday in fact,' said his hostess, closing the door, 'and you were there!'

SIR HUGH CASSON

When I was about eighteen I went to the grandest dinner party at Londonderry House in London that I had ever attended. There were about 150 people, distinguished guests for the coronation of George VI. All kinds of royalty and heads of state. I was trying to make conversation with a rather stuffy girl and said, 'Who is that pompous-looking ass with a moustache opposite?' 'My father,' she replied. I searched desperately the length of the endless table. There was not another man with a moustache.

DUKE OF BEDFORD

On the day in December 1988 when Edwina Currie resigned her ministerial position at the Department of Health, I was to address Britain's largest indoor lunch – at least we all thought it the largest.

As a partial vegetarian, I refused the meat and asked for an omelette. After being introduced to 1597 highway engineers at the Institute of Highways and Transportation Christmas Lunch, I thanked the president for the egg meal. It may not sound much now. That day it was a fine topical joke. I explained that I ate many eggs and expected to eat more if they came down in price. My speech then concerned topics associated with roads in London.

A newspaper, the *Daily Telegraph* I think, covered the egg remarks and was sub-edited to make me appear against eggs. I soon received a letter from an egg producer, who explained in explicit, blunt language that he had stopped being a lifelong Conservative after reading my disappointing comments. Five pages.

Once a week I like to ring someone who writes to me, sometimes to thank them for a good letter making constructive suggestions, or for offering constructive criticism. In this case I wanted to make it clear that a vote should not be lost through a misunderstanding.

I dialled. A woman answered. 'May I please speak to Mr P.J. Anyname?' She called 'Paul'. A man came to the telephone. I explained who I was. He asked if he could say something. I asked him to wait. Had he been at the lunch? Had he been a witness with the rest of that record lot of lunchers who had heard me testify to eggs and to all associated with them? Did he realise that in five years of community service as a minister I had never read a letter so undeserved? Mistakes I made but that speech had not been one of them.

All through, he tried to break in. Eventually he succeeded. He said: 'My brother's name is Peter. He wrote the letter. I didn't.'

I asked him to pass on my fondest greetings!

PETER BOTTOMLEY

One of the first big dinner parties I went to when I left school was given at Arlington House by the fabulously rich Lady Michelham.

About thirty people sat down at a huge table covered in orchids and set with gold plates. I had never even seen gold plates before, let alone eaten off them!

The first course was a slice of cantaloup melon and I picked up a gold spoon, but at the first touch the melon leapt off the plate and disappeared under the table.

I sat crimson with embarrassment while it was retrieved by a disdainful footman with powdered hair, and another piece placed in front of me!

BARBARA CARTLAND

I was invited to a State Department dinner at the White House under President Lyndon B. Johnson. I happened to be in the east by myself and so I took the shuttle from New York to Washington, DC. I checked myself into the Madison Hotel. When it was time I put on my dinner jacket and because it was a lovely evening, I decided to stroll over to the White House.

When I got to the entrance one of the guards stationed there said 'Your card, please!' I thought he said, 'Your *car* please!' I looked at him strangely and said, 'I have no car!' He said, 'Then you can't come in here!' I said, 'That's silly!' He said, 'Silly or not, you need a card!' (I am still hearing *car*!) A little annoyed, I said, 'You mean if I left and came back with a car it would be all right to come in?' He said, 'Yes!' I then said, 'Why didn't my invitation say so?' He said, 'What invitation?' I said, 'This one!' taking it out of my pocket. He smiled and said, 'Please come in!'

SAMMY CAHN

I was drawing cartoons for a business seminar at Old Trafford one Saturday, the idea being the business persons could take their cartoons home afterwards. United were playing Spurs after the seminar and we could all go and watch the game. There was also to be a buffet at half-time.

At half-time everyone stood up and went for the buffet. I stayed in my seat, unsure whether or not to follow. After some thought I decided to go and join them. I went into a room crowded with people and full of tables with food on them. I walked over to one table surrounded by chaps and picked up a pie from one of the plates. Everyone went quiet and stared at me as I took a bite from the pie.

'Oi. That's my pie you're eating!' said one angry fellow.

'Er . . . isn't this a buffet?' I said.

'No, it bloody well isn't!' he blurted.

I looked around the room. I didn't recognize a single face.

'I paid for that pie,' he said.

'Sorry,' I said. Putting the half-eaten pie back on his plate I backed away from the angry glares and disappeared into the crowd. As I came out of the room I noticed the business lot pouring out of the room next door.

TONY HUSBAND

A SLIP OF
THE TONGUE . . .

BOB MONKHOUSE
LUDOVIC KENNEDY
BILLY DAINTY
JIM BOWEN

Reading the autocue I said, '007 James Bond looked round for a gents.' I should have said 'agents'. You know how they say wisest people learn from the mistakes of others? I am one of the others.

BOB MONKHOUSE

Once when reading the news on ITN in around 1956-7, I had to refer to the Liverpool Chamber of Shipping. Unfortunately I put two 't's where the two 'p's should have been. Luckily, hardly anyone noticed.

LUDOVIC KENNEDY

The only boob I can think of was in this show *Verse and Chorus*. I was supposed to say, 'This is my latest book – *Under a Bridge with Dick and Harry.*'

Roy Hudd looks and says, '*Unabridged Dictionary*'.

But opening night I said, 'Under a dick with bridge and Harry!'

I can still hear the laughs.

BILLY DAINTY

When the very first series of *Bullseye* games was being recorded, I asked one of the contestants what he did for a living. His reply was, 'I've been unemployed for six months,' to which I replied, 'Smashing!'

Can't get it more wrong than that.

JIM BOWEN

GOD GIVEN . . .

THE REVEREND THE LORD SOPER

MARTI CAINE

THE ARCHBISHOP OF CANTERBURY

THE ARCHBISHOP OF ARMAGH

13

One Wednesday, during an open-air meeting on Tower Hill, we were discussing alcoholism and the effect of prohibition in the USA in the 1920s. A heckler was describing with lurid details the dreadful effects of the 18th Amendment in America. I asked him: 'Have you been to America?'

'No.'

Then I said rather truculently: 'Don't talk of things you know nothing about.'

Whereupon a well-known atheist asked: 'Have you ever been to Heaven?'

'No.'

Then said he: 'Don't *you* talk of things you know nothing about.'

THE REVEREND THE LORD SOPER

The anecdote concerns my youngest son, Max. He was five at the time and during the Parent-Teacher evening, just before the Christmas holidays, we were studying the nativity pictures around the walls of the classroom. 'That's my picture,' said Max, and upon examining this work of art I discovered, along with the normal nativity characters, a huge fat man in the middle of the picture.

I said, 'I can see Mary, Joseph and baby Jesus, and the three wise men, but who's the big fat man in the middle?' and Max said, 'That's Round John Virgin.'

MARTI CAINE

The Archbishop of Canterbury and Terry Waite had gone to Heathrow to meet Bishop Desmond Tutu arriving from New York on Concorde. So had not a few reporters and TV camera crews. All were gathered at the mouth of the tunnel leading from the aircraft into the special reception area.

With typical modesty Desmond Tutu was chatting to other passengers, and to crew members, on board the aircraft. He disembarked almost last of all. Groups of bemused passengers were emerging meantime to find themselves face to face with the Archbishop of Canterbury in glistening purple, and brilliantly lit by the TV lights. Some were plainly troubled. Was the End of the World at hand?

Terry, equal to any occasion, stepped forward and remarked in tones of authority, 'Please don't be upset. The Archbishop of Canterbury meets the Concorde flight from New York every Friday afternoon as a matter of routine . . .'

THE ARCHBISHOP OF CANTERBURY

On one occasion, when preaching at a service for several hundred young people and their parents, I felt it was a good opportunity to draw their attention to a new window which had been placed in the church the previous week. My great mistake was to try and involve the children in the sermon! I asked the question: 'What is different about church today compared with last Sunday?'

Complete silence.

I tried again.

'Now children, stand up on mummy's knee and take a good look round church, and when you see what is different compared to last Sunday please put up your hands.'

Suddenly a little hand in the back row shot into the air and a voice called out for all to hear:

'Please sir, there aren't as many out as there were last Sunday!'

THE ARCHBISHOP OF ARMAGH

YOUR ROYAL HIGHNESS . . .

SIR PETER SCOTT

HAMMOND INNES

SHEILA HANCOCK

PAT BOONE

DORA BRYAN

RICHARD TODD

ALAN TITCHMARSH

In 1947 I was engaged by the BBC to be one of the commentators for the wedding of Princess Elizabeth to the Duke of Edinburgh. My station was on the roof of St Margaret's, Westminster, overlooking the entrance to Westminster Abbey. The assistant who was delegated to look after me and see that the equipment was in working order was a then unknown member of the BBC staff, Rex Alston. I was, as usual, extremely nervous. I remember the voice of 'Lobby' Lotbiniere, the Director of Outside Broadcasts, coming over the line from Broadcasting House to all the commentators just before the programme started: 'Good luck, boys. Don't forget this is the largest listening audience there has ever been for any broadcast, 250 million people will be listening to you.' Surprisingly this did not add anything to my peace of mind. A few moments later Rex trod on the junction box of the headphones, cutting off our direct communication. Quickly we switched on the portable radio and were just in time to take our cue from that.

The Royal Wedding was my second post-war attempt at commentary. The first had been the Victory Procession, in which I had travelled in naval uniform in a DUKW amphibious vehicle. I was required to do three short periods of commentary, one somewhere in south London, another as we came through Parliament Square and the third as we passed the saluting base. Here, with my cap sitting slightly crooked on my head because of the headphones that I wore beneath it, I had saluted my King. The worst which befell me that day was in Parliament Square where I could not find an adequate word to describe the decorative pagoda-like structure which had been set up in the middle of it. As we came past I fought for words to describe it, trying without success to avoid using the one which first came to mind. On the following day *The Times* reported that 'Words failed Mr Scott when he came to describe the ceremonial erection in

Parliament Square'.

SIR PETER SCOTT

(Excerpt from *The Eye of the Wind* by Sir Peter Scott,
        published by Hodder and Stoughton, 1961.)

It was at one of those Buckingham Palace luncheons.
Somebody had had the good sense to put me next to
Princess Anne so that we were able to find common
ground in sailing. It was afterwards, as I went through
into the drawing room, that I found myself in company
with one of the corgis. I bent down to pat it.

Now anybody who has owned dogs all their life is in-
evitably very attuned to the moulting stage, which in
bitches occurs twice a year just before they go on heat –
'getting ready for the boys', we always call it.

I was in the doorway at the moment of finding my
hand entangled with dog's hairs and as I straightened up,
I found the Queen right behind me, and without thinking I said 'Your dog's moulting.'

She gave me a stare out of those electric blue eyes of
hers, but then made the sort of exclamation of alarm any
dog owner would have made.

Dogs' hairs are no respecters of persons, but I did feel
I should have kept my mouth shut and let her find out for
herself. Apparently my *faux pas* was not taken very
seriously as she spent the last quarter of an hour talking
to Wynford Vaughan-Thomas and myself about the in-
security of police helmets and how on VE Day she had
gone outside the Palace railings, mingled with the
crowd, and in the excitement of the moment had
knocked one of the bobbies' helmets off.

HAMMOND INNES

To my surprise, I had been invited to have lunch with the Queen and Prince Philip. These little get-togethers are presumably to keep the Royal Family in touch with their subjects' points of view, which on that occasion, coming as they did from a man from the DHSS, a rabbi and me, were pretty diverse. Over the brandy snaps, we discussed vandalism which Prince Philip strenuously deplored. I found myself protesting boldly: 'Well, it's all right for you, love, living 'ere.'

My carefully RADA-trained voice is apt to lapse into its natural accent – only more so – when I feel inadequate. At the same lunch, I should have learned a lesson in graciousness from the Queen who, when I inadvertently trod on one of her corgis, ignored its yelp and calmed my confusion by saying: 'It's her own fault. She shouldn't be the same colour as the carpet.'

I usually keep very quiet about my OBE – partly because I think it was a mistake and they might take it back, and partly because I made such an idiot of myself when I received it. First, I went in my clapped out MG which made an unholy row in the courtyard of Buckingham Palace, and then I yelped in panic, waving my naked hands at the smooth major-domo when he instructed us to keep our gloves on if the Queen wore hers. Visions of soiling Her Majesty's immaculate kid leather with my sweaty, bare skin appalled me until a sweet housemaid hissed at me from behind a pillar, proffering a pair of immaculate white ones. Designer John Bates would have killed me if he had seen their startling brightness against the subtle greys and beiges of the outfit he had lent me for the occasion, although he did resignedly accept the huge holes that another equerry had to drill into the pigskin jacket to put a pin in to allow the Queen to hang my medal. Once inside the impressive investiture hall I forgot all the instructions, leapt forward too soon and practically caused them to call out the guard to protect the Queen from a suspected assassin.

SHEILA HANCOCK

(Excerpts from *Ramblings of an Actress* by Sheila Hancock, published by Hutchinson)

A Royal Command Performance is certainly one of the most pressure packed and important 'high points' in any entertainer's career. As I prepared for my second Royal Command Performance in London, the première of *West Side Story*, I tried to be very calm and blasé about the whole thing, actually snickering and poking fun at some of the other performers who were so visibly nervous. Those performers included Claudia Cardinale, Peter Finch, and a host of others.

I kept saying to them, 'The Queen is just a woman, a woman with an important job of course, but just a flesh and blood human being like you and me. Why are you so nervous?' I thought I had my nerves completely under control, and everything in perspective.

The big moment came, as all the entertainers and notables were lined up in the big reception room, and the Queen and her entourage entered the far end of the room. I was down towards the end of the line, and still was somewhat amused as the Queen began to make her way towards us (I was between Peter and Claudia). I mentally rehearsed the protocol, what I was supposed to say when I bowed slightly to her, and kept reminding myself I was an American, and not a British subject anyway.

Soon she was talking to Peter on my left, and I suddenly felt the flutter of nerves. Then she moved to stand in front of me. I bowed slightly and said, 'Your Royal Highness' as I was supposed to, and looked into her eyes. To my absolute and utter amazement, she said,

'We've met before.'

I was paralysed, because it had never entered my mind she would remember that we had met once before at a previous Command Performance when I had actually performed musically. I suppose royalty is briefed before these things, and she simply took the wind out of my sails by that pronouncement. I stammered, 'We did?' (Imagine appearing not to remember having met the Queen!)

She said 'Yes, you came over for another Command Performance, and if I remember correctly, interrupted your studies at school to do it.' Of course, she was right, but my apparent lapse of memory and my nervousness caused her face to begin to twitch. Thinking back, it was probably a reaction to my own face twitching, which I became aware of at that point.

She stood looking at me for what seemed a couple of hours, and I realized my mouth was hanging open and I wasn't saying anything, but that I probably looked as if I was about to. Both our faces were twitching, and I realized I must say something, but my mind was blank. I finally said, 'I'm glad you're here – '

I said to the Queen of England, in London at her own Command Performance, that I was glad she was there. I imagine it was the dumbest thing anyone has ever said to her, though I'm quite sure other dumb things have been said under the pressure of moments like that. I really expect that these are gruelling experiences for the Royal Family, because of the tension other people feel in their presence.

Anyway, a picture appeared the next day in all the London papers of the Queen standing before Pat Boone, with his mouth hanging open and a completely dumbstruck look on his face.

PAT BOONE

I was rather nervous about the visit to the Palace, and pondered for ages about what to wear, finally settling for a smart little brown dress and small mink hat. It did not make things any easier when I discovered that I was the only female present – apart from the Queen, of course. No one showed me the ladies room, and I left my coat and hat in a very ordinary room, considering it was Buckingham Palace. It contained several children's bicycles and had no mirror, so I just had to hope that my lipstick wasn't smudged and that my slip wasn't showing when we were ushered into an ante-room for sherry. There I was standing around with five men I didn't know. It was quite daunting. Then in came four corgis, who broke the tension, followed by the Queen and Prince Philip. They did their best to make us feel at home, but how can anyone be completely relaxed on such an occasion? I knelt down to greet a corgi when he trotted into the room, so at least I didn't have far to go in order to curtsy to the Queen. I was on the floor when she came in.

It was all wonderful, of course, but I just wished everyone would go away so that I could have a quiet look around the Palace. There were so many beautiful things to see, and anyway, I wanted to find a loo. Somehow I didn't relax at all. I sat next to Prince Philip at lunch. It was a very good lunch, what I can remember of it, but when the fresh fruit came round I declined. Then a large gold plate of grapes came round, complete with a neat pair of gold scissors to serve them with. I thought I could risk some grapes, so I cut myself what I thought was a dainty clump. There were far more attached to the stalk than I had anticipated, and my judgement hadn't been very good. When they were reposing on my plate I was horrified to see that they looked as though they weighed at least a pound. But one has to rise to such occasions with dignity, so I discreetly and daintily chomped my way through them as though it was quite a normal every-day occurrence for me to eat a pound of grapes at one sit-ting. The pips were a bit of a problem. To have filled my plate with pips would simply have drawn attention to the number of grapes I'd eaten, and as you can't drop them on the carpet under the table at Buckingham Palace, or blow them across the room, there was only one alterna-tive. I swallowed them all.

DORA BRYAN

(Excerpt from *According to Dora* published by The Bodley Head)

The high spot of 1947 for us came when we were invited to perform for the Royal Family at Balmoral. The Coun-tess of Airlie, a lady-in-waiting to the Queen, was a regular supporter of the rep. She had found that I had been an officer in the regiment of which the Queen was Colonel-in-Chief, and wrote to me asking if I could go to Balmoral Castle one weekend to see if I thought a full-scale performance there would be feasible.

I determined to arrive in style. As I had no car then, I hired a local Rolls-Royce that I had seen about the town in various wedding and funeral processions. When I explained the purpose to its owner, I got it for a very moderate sum for the day – a Sunday.

As I drew up outside the castle itself I wondered what door I should head for – was I a tradesman relegated to the kitchen entrance or a visitor entitled to go in by the front door? I got out and dithered for a few moments, and it was then that I noticed for the first time the large plate on the back of the car bearing the sign 'HACK-NEY CARRIAGE'.

Before I could do anything about it the front door opened and a man came to greet me. He was a household official who had been expecting me, and was polite enough not to notice the fallen status of my vehicle. I was taken to look at the ballroom and some adjacent rooms that would be usable as dressing-rooms, and I gave my opinion that a fully-staged play could be done in the ballroom. Even if I had had any doubts, I would not have voiced them.

Soon after, we received a formal invitation and Barbara Borrow, our scenic designer, went to the castle to draw up her plans.

The play was to be *At Mrs Beams*, a rather awful boarding-house comedy, so far as I can remember.

When the day came, we were all taken by coach to Balmoral. Soon after we arrived the Queen herself very charmingly thanked us for coming and said she was greatly looking forward to the evening.

After the performance, which seemed to go down quite well, we were led to a meal that had been prepared for us, and then invited to join the Royals in the drawing-room for drinks.

There was quite a family gathering: all our own Royal Family (am I right in remembering that Princess Elizabeth had just become engaged to Prince Philip of Greece?) were present and several other foreign Royals also. It says much for their charm and easy grace that we felt quite at home and chattered away happily.

Then came my moment of utter confusion.

With all the excitement, I had neglected to attend to the needs of nature. Fuelled by generous quantities of wine with supper and a massive whisky now in my hand, I suddenly reckoned there was not a moment to lose. Aware that one should not leave the room without some sort of royal assent, I edged over to Peter Townsend, who was then the equerry on duty, and confided my problem. Mercifully, he was a quick thinker.

He said it would be perfectly all right to slip out and indicated a door at the end of the room. 'Go out there,' he said. 'Right across the hall you will see a door. That's usually only used by the King himself, but it leads to a cloakroom. Be quick, and you'll be OK.'

I scurried into the hallowed royal loo in the nick of time, and stood in shuddering relief at a urinal. (That seems hardly the right nomenclature for the plumbing facilities in such august premises.)

Many seconds later I was still in full spate when, to my absolute horror, the monarch himself hurried in. Now, to my knowledge, there is no manual of etiquette or protocol that deals with this particular situation. All sorts of solutions raced through my head. Should I bow politely and carry on unperturbed, or should I hurriedly apologise and retreat? What on earth was I to do?

As he stood beside me, I thought I detected a slight flicker in the King's jaw muscles, often the prelude to conversation made difficult by his speech impediment. After what seemed an eternity, however, he said nothing and I eventually managed to cut off my water supply. Fumbling with shaking fingers at my buttons (we had no zips in those days) I backed away, still in silence. Anxious to retreat as quickly as I could, I nevertheless took a few moments to swill my hands at the wash-basin, not wishing to seem ignorant of personal hygiene.

Then, remembering what I had seen of court behaviour in various Hollywood films, I proceeded to back out of the cloakroom, bowing as I reached the door, and then fled, sweating with embarrassment, back to the drawing-room.

RICHARD TODD

(Excerpt from *Caught in the Act* by Richard Todd, published by Century Hutchinson, 1986)

In the days of *Breakfast Time* when the red sofa ruled supreme, I'd just finished a 'live' gardening item, during which I extolled the virtues of manure – having taken along a bucket of the stuff and pushed my hands into it to show how crumbly and delectable it was. The programme credits rolled and I started to scrape this wonderful brown soil enrichment from my hands, only to hear the programme producer saying to some unseen person, 'Don't shake hands with him, you've seen where they've been.'

I looked up in time to see the Princess of Wales walking towards me with hands outstretched. We met with a gentle squidge and, as our hands parted, the only thing I could think of to say was, 'I'll never wash again.'

ALAN TITCHMARSH

TRAINS AND BOATS AND PLANES . . .

GARY WILMOT

PATRICK MOORE

MAGGIE MOONE

NORRIS McWHIRTER

ROY HATTERSLEY

MARK CURRY

DANA

I was on my way to a gig and had to stop for a nature call; when I got back to the car I found I had locked the keys in; it was pouring with rain and numerous people stopped and tried to help and indeed eventually one person walked around to the passenger door and opened it! Quite embarrassing in front of a lot of people brandishing anything from wire hangers to iron bars, and there was a lot of debate!

GARY WILMOT

I was passing through Utah, in the United States, and stopped briefly at a hostelry for a coffee or something. There were various people there. One of them came up to me, and after establishing that I was a stranger he said: 'This is our Mormon state. It's different from the rest of the US. You'll find no smoking, swearing, drinking or wild women here.'

I made the tactless reply: 'Hardly worth coming, is it?'
After that, nobody would speak to me any more!

PATRICK MOORE

In 1986 I was travelling north on the M1, due to start rehearsals for the *Russ Abbott Show* at the North Pier Theatre, Blackpool. I was alone and drove into Watford Gap service area to refuel. I happily filled the tank, paid my bill and then continued my journey . . . that is, for a quarter of a mile, until my car chugged to a halt! Not knowing the first thing about car mechanics, I had no idea what the problem was. I contacted the AA, and also my husband, who immediately got in his car to 'rescue' me. The AA man and my husband arrived simultaneously and it was soon discovered, to my embarrassment, that I'd filled the tank full of diesel and not petrol!! It proved to be a very expensive mistake! The AA man, however, thought it was very amusing and asked for a signed photo as a memento!

MAGGIE MOONE

When, at the outbreak of war, it was expected that the civilian population would be heavily bombed by the *Luftwaffe*, I was 'evacuated' along with my two brothers to a sleepy little village in Hampshire. The house in which we stayed was owned by a lady who is now a quite famous countess. The maid in the house was very depressed about her enormous girth.

Because of severe petrol rationing an expedition to the shops in Andover was quite an event. Sitting beside the countess in the front seat, Maisie caused the car to list heavily to port. As we came round a bend we saw two enormous women standing beside the bus stop. 'Maisie,' said the countess, 'cheer up and be thankful that compared with those two ladies you are really quite slim.' 'That's me mum, ma'am,' said Maisie. Quick as a flash the countess rejoined, 'Oh, I don't mean her, I mean the enormous lady standing next to her.' 'That's me sister, ma'am,' said Maisie, and silence prevailed until we reached the shops in Andover.

NORRIS McWHIRTER

Believe it or not, Clive Jenkins was the star of the Monty Python sketch that brought down the curtain on the first half of the recent Amnesty International Charity Gala. He played the 'mystery guest' on an imaginary television quiz show in which bound and blindfolded contestants won handsome prizes if they guessed the identity of a visiting celebrity who kicked, punched and generally knocked hell out of them.

Apparently, Clive performed superbly. Carping

critics may say that his triumph was no more than the outcome of shrewd typecasting. But when I saw pictures of Mr Jenkins putting his polished and pointed Chelsea boot in I could only feel regret that I had refused an invitation to do the same on an earlier night.

I had no sense of guilt. The Gala was a sell-out, with or without my trivial participation. I had no feeling of lost opportunity. I learned many years ago that politicians who do ridiculous things in public with the hope of appearing warm and lovable never look warm and lovable but only ridiculous. But as I looked at the pictures of the willingly pinioned victims awaiting with obvious pleasure the collision of Mr Jenkins's pointed toe-cap with the tender parts of their anatomy, I was overcome with a single simple conviction: into each life some farce must fall. And how much better if it can be exorcised on stage in aid of a good cause rather than in real life, on, say – to take a single humiliating example – New Street Station, Birmingham.

I have alighted on New Street's concrete platform (remembering 'to take my hand baggage with me') at least once a week since the lovely red brick of Snow Hill was pounded into the ground to make a smooth surface for a car-park. And my problem has never been leaving luggage behind but bringing too much with me.

During the transient days of ministerial office I travelled between London and Birmingham loaded down like a nineteenth-century Kowloon coolie. I could only manage it at all if every bag and parcel was suspended from me with the precision of a Guggenheim mobile.

My right elbow I kept close to my side, bent in an exact right-angle so that my forearm stuck out precisely parallel to the ground. A suit-bag over my shoulder and hooked to my right hand pulled my forearm upwards.

But a ministerial red box clutched tightly in the same fist pulled my arm down and kept the Euclidian aberration in perfect balance. In my other hand I carried a suitcase, the weight of which kept my left arm rigidly and vertically by my side, ensuring that the briefcase of constituency correspondence squashed between it and my rib-cage could not escape. My ticket I trapped between thumb and suitcase handle.

It was quite impossible to lift it to the level of the ticket-collector's outstretched palm. But most NUR members were kind enough to reach down and take it from me, and all preferred the thumbtrap technique to the alternative – carrying the ticket in my mouth and either blowing it to them as I passed their box or offering it from between my lips like a bird returning to the nest with a worm for its fledgling.

I tried to reconcile myself to the weight, inconvenience and risibility of my complicated load by thinking of the whole procedure as a health-giving combination of Canadian Air Force callisthenics and Tibetan yoga. But I could never complete the exercise with the degree of casual nonchalance that ought to typify the behaviour of a man with a Harvard suit-bag. Frankly, I had to concentrate very hard to move at all. No doubt it was the effort of moving forward that prevented me from noticing the packing-case that was rattling and shaking at the other end of the platform.

It was when the shaking turned to a shudder and the planks that made up its front and sides collapsed that I first became aware of the goose. But by the time it stepped out of the debris my attention was fully engaged. My first, distant thought was that there was a man inside. As a child of the twentieth century, I suspected a publicity stunt. As a child of Yorkshire, I wondered if geese travelled more cheaply than people and if this was an elaborate way of defrauding the railway. Then it drew near and I realised it was the work of God, not man: a goose's goose, the sort of goose that sensible swans would like to be.

The goose walked towards me, perfectly goose-shaped, like a four-foot pear covered in feathers. It was a well-adjusted goose that walked calmly and with self-possession in regular paces, not high stepping idiotically like a German soldier. It looked neither to left nor right, but moved with enviable certainty towards the first-class waiting-room.

I have always thought of the goose as a benign bird that lays golden eggs, flies up surburban sitting-room walls and saves the Capitol. A small boy, attempting to smash a chocolate machine, must have been to the wrong pantomimes, subscribed to a more sophisticated school of interior decoration and lacked a classical education. He was terrified by the goose, and ran screaming to his mother, colliding in his flight with a massive tin tumbril used by British Rail to carry Red Star parcels from train to post office. By unhappy chance his impact released its brake. The juggernaut began to roll slowly towards me, down the platform incline. It quickly gained pace.

By this time my hands were totally atrophied, approaching the stage when failure of blood supply produces either gangrene or frostbite, or both. But I did not lose my nerve. Lifting my left foot I diverted the rogue wheelbarrow into a pile of mail sacks where it no doubt remained for several days. But my pleasure in the passage of athletic, indeed balletic, self-defence was dimmed by my failure to keep hold of my ticket. It spun from my right hand and landed on the line between train and platform.

But I was, after all, in Birmingham, the city I had represented in Parliament for well over a decade. If I could not talk my way through the barrier here . . . So I advanced to the ticket-collector and boldly announced, 'I am Roy Hattersley.' His reply – 'Well done' – was less than encouraging, but I pressed on. 'I have no ticket,' I confessed. The subsequent long silence destroyed my remaining confidence. I rushed in to fill the verbal vacuum.

'London train . . . platform six . . . weighed down with luggage . . . packing case shaking . . . split open . . . great big goose . . . three feet tall . . . grey . . . four feet tall . . . perfectly amiable . . . five feet tall . . . little boy . . . very frightened . . . screamed and shouted . . . crashed into lorry . . . released brake . . . at least forty miles an hour . . . nasty accident . . . stopped with foot . . . look at mark on shoe . . . ticket fell on line. Recovering it would be both dangerous and illegal.'

The ticket-collector was a reasonable and compassionate man. In any case, the queue building up behind me had begun to turn ugly. 'OK, squire,' he said. 'On your way this time. But if it happens again you'll have to pay.'

ROY HATTERSLEY

(Reproduced from *Politics Apart* by Roy Hattersley, with the permission of BBC Enterprises Ltd)

Once I was getting off a train in Wakefield, Yorkshire. The train was stopping before continuing straight on to London. As I was getting off, the man in front of me was struggling with some suitcases. I thought I would be helpful and asked if I could take the case in front of me off the train for him: it was very big and heavy. He nodded at me so I struggled off.

I strained and heaved with the case all the way down the platform and through the ticket barrier. The man gestured for me to follow him to the car park, which I did. I even managed the case to his car, where I let it go with relief. He asked me where my car was parked; I replied that my car wasn't there. He then looked puzzled and asked me what I was going to do with my case. *My* case! I said it *wasn't* my case; he said it *wasn't* his. Panic, worry, embarrassment! It was all a great misunderstanding. The man thought I was asking him if I could take my case off the train seeing as he had finished with his. I told the ticket guard this story and I just hope that someone somewhere isn't looking for their belongings to this day!!!

MARK CURRY

Just after Eurovision I did my first European tour (each night a different city and country). We arrived in Venice (I thought) and I decided to kill time before the show by going to see the gondolas. I went to the hotel receptionist and asked him to direct me to them. He looked very puzzled and asked me to repeat the question. When I did repeat it he looked even *more* puzzled. I was extremely tired and felt it was rather silly to hire a receptionist who couldn't speak English.

In desperation I said, 'Just direct me to the nearest canal.' After thinking for a moment he said he thought there was one canal up in the mountains.

It dawned on me that something was very wrong. 'Where am I?' I asked.

Well, I was in Vienna!

DANA

MY LORDS, LADIES
AND GENTLEMEN . . .

Roy Hudd

Cyril Fletcher

Odette M.C. Hallowes

David Blunkett

Sir Vivian Fuchs

I opened a garden fête years ago. The lady who organized it was called Pat Fowe and, at the end of my speech when I had thanked everyone connected with the fête, I said, 'And, of course, very special thanks must go to the lady who arranged today's marvellous event – Fat Cow.' She was a large lady too!

ROY HUDD

My wife and I once opened two fêtes on one Saturday afternoon when we were appearing in a summer show at Bournemouth. My wife made an impassioned plea for Dr Barnardo's when she should have spoken for the Royal Society for the Prevention of Cruelty to Animals. We wondered why the audience looked a little blanker than usual!

CYRIL FLETCHER

The film *Odette* had its charity French première at the Opéra in Paris before President Auriol of France. It was shown to a distinguished audience, many of whom had worked in the Resistance. The Opéra is a spectacular theatre with a large awe-inspiring auditorium, especially when viewed from the stage.

At the end of the film, the director, Herbert Wilcox, said I should go on the stage and say a few words. The enormous curtain was drawn back, and I then realized the vast size of the stage and auditorium and felt very small standing there all alone on centre stage.

I looked towards the president's box and suddenly saw him stand up, followed by the audience. I thought: 'They are leaving. What shall I do now?' Everyone then began to applaud, which made me even more nervous and embarrassed.

I remained speechless, but looking down at my feet I

saw the faces of the electricians in the prompter's box. Seeing my hesitation, they said to me, 'Go on, you were not afraid of the Germans, so do not be afraid of them!'

It was thanks to those electricians that I was able to surmount a most anxious and embarrassing moment.

ODETTE M.C. HALLOWES

When I was a teenager I liked to speak out on behalf of others whether they wanted me to or not. On one occasion, we had made a trip from school to a nearby youth club where we were given refreshments, generally entertained and made to feel we were part of the real world rather than the separate environment of the boarding school from which we had come.

As everyone knew I was the one who liked to do the spouting, I was asked if I would say a word or two of thanks. I readily agreed and reached out on the counter for what I presumed was the microphone. Picking up the shapely object unfamiliar to one from the sheltered existence of the School for the Blind, I raised it to my lips and addressed the audience. It didn't seem to work. The truth then dawned – I was addressing the assembled throng, not through a microphone, but through a Coca-Cola bottle! You can't win them all.

DAVID BLUNKETT

Before my departure after giving a lecture, the chairwoman offered me a cheque. 'Oh, no,' said I, 'it is quite unnecessary.' She then asked if she could use it for one of the society's projects. When I asked what the project was she replied, 'Oh! it's a fund to help us get better speakers in future.' Collapse of personal ego!

SIR VIVIAN FUCHS

HITTING THE RIGHT NOTE . . .

NEIL KINNOCK

CHRISTOPHER CHATAWAY

THE SHADOWS

HARRY SECOMBE

VINCE HILL

At the University of Wales Inter-College Eisteddfod in 1965, the University College Cardiff Choir (under our conductor Owain Arwel Hughes) sang the great chorus from *Tannhäuser*.

On the second 'Alleluia', three of us singing first bass fell off the chairs on which we were precariously balanced, without breaking a note. We continued without the benefit of seeing the conductor. And our choir won the competition.

I'm probably one of the three people alive who laughs when I hear Wagner . . .

NEIL KINNOCK

I was staying recently in a rather smart hotel in Melbourne. As I went to bed I was aware of music coming from the room next door. I knocked quite gently on the wall to indicate that it was unacceptably loud.

I must nonetheless have dropped off to sleep. At 2.0 a.m. I was wide awake and the music from next door seemed even louder. I walked out into the corridor to get the room number. I then telephoned the next-door room. A sleepy Australian voice replied and I told him in no uncertain terms that his music was disgracefully loud. Another ten minutes and the noise was no better. I rang again, even more angry this time. Still no improvement.

I telephoned the hotel security. The noise seemed to get even worse. I banged more angrily upon the wall.

Eventually the hotel security men arrived. 'Come in,' I said. 'Just listen to the level of this music. It really is impossible to sleep.' The two extremely polite hotel officials entered my room, walked to the side of the bed and turned a knob. There was silence. All the time it had been my own radio with its loudspeaker by the wall which had been the cause of the trouble.

In the morning I slunk quietly out of the hotel, hoping not to meet a bleary-eyed Australian complaining of a night's sleep ruined by calls from some demented Englishman.

CHRISTOPHER CHATAWAY

Just three years after their first hit the Shadows were to lose their third member, and while it was being strongly hinted from various quarters that with only twenty-five per cent of the original line-up remaining maybe it was time for a name change, another bombshell was dropped.

After the summer season, Licorice had found himself at a personal crossroads. He was already a Jehovah's Witness when he joined the group, and as Brian Bennett had also been of the same faith for a short while, when years before he'd attended meetings with his mother, it was easy for him to understand the strong feelings Licorice had about his beliefs.

An increasing amount of his time was being spent preaching from door to door and attending meetings. It was gradually taking over his life and causing a few raised eyebrows within the group.

I was really the middle man between Licorice and the other two. I felt that it was up to me to explain to him that he couldn't turn up late just because he was talking to someone about the Bible.

I conceded that it was a great thing to do, to want to seek the truth, but on the other hand the job had to be done, so I told him that he'd have to do some soul-searching and come to a decision. Licorice announced his departure from the Shadows in October, as *Shindig* was sitting comfortably in a Top 10 headed by Brian Poole and the Tremeloes' *Do You Love Me?*

It was a black autumn for the Shadows' fans; Bruce was leaving, Licorice was leaving and after a great year for former members Jet and Tony, during which they notched three Top 10 hits as a duo, Jet was in hospital after a bad car crash.

Despite his impending departure, Bruce was as desperate as the others to find a replacement for Licorice. Hank had ideas too, as he told the press:

> We may give an audition to a promising boy called *Paul McCartney* in an unknown group called the Beatles. Come to think of it he won't do, he's from Liverpool. We want a lad from Newcastle-upon-Tyne – the more Geordies in the band the better!

THE SHADOWS

(Excerpt from *The Story of the Shadows* by Mike Reed, published by Elm Tree Books/Hamish Hamilton)

One of his worst *faux pas* was the time he was giving a concert at Wormwood Scrubs Prison and he sang 'Bless This House'. He was fine until he got to the line 'Bless these walls so firm and stout keeping want and trouble out', when he and the entire audience erupted in howls of laughter!

JENNY SECOMBE ON HARRY SECOMBE

One story that comes to mind happened years ago when I'd just recorded 'Edelweiss' and it was at the top of the charts. I was playing in a northern club one night, I'd had a fabulous evening – the audience loved the show and I got a standing ovation; and as I came off stage and made my way to the dressing room some chap stopped me and said, 'Hey, if you'd have recorded Edelweiss instead of Engelbert Humperdinck, then you'd have had a hit with it!' – I ask you, what do you do?

VINCE HILL

ACCIDENTS WILL HAPPEN . . .

TERRY WOGAN

SHIRLEY WILLIAMS

SIR GEORG SOLTI

CHRISTOPHER TIMOTHY

TERRY SCOTT

JONATHAN DIMBLEBY

I well remember Monday 18 February 1985 – it was the first evening of the new thrice-weekly *Wogan* which comes live from the BBC Television Theatre at Shepherd's Bush.

One of my guests was Elton John. I left my chair to walk over to greet Elton who was standing by the piano, went to shake hands, tripped, not very elegantly, and ended up on the floor with Elton trying to bring me to my feet. After several jolly japes from Elton I regained my composure (I think) and we carried on with the show.

Not a very auspicious start to a new series, but it certainly made the papers the next day and, much to my mortification, guests coming on to *Wogan* still remind me of that first evening which to this day brings a flush to the old cheeks!

TERRY WOGAN

I was a bit short of money to buy toothpaste, T-shirts and soft drinks back in my days as a student at Colombia, so it was necessary to find a job. I'd done a bit of speaking for B'nai Brith, and they kindly found me part-time work with El Al in New York.

At that time, the state of Israel produced one new issue of beautifully designed stamps after another, which were sold in vast quantities to wealthy stamp collectors. It looked like money for old (or rather, new) rope. My job was to count out the pages of stamps and send them to the collectors.

It took time counting. One day, exasperated by my own slowness, I licked my thumb to count more quickly. Three minutes later, a hundred pages of priceless new stamps were glued inextricably together. I was sacked on the spot – the only friend of Israel to raise negative funds for the cause.

SHIRLEY WILLIAMS

In 1976, as part of the United States' Bicentennial celebrations, the Paris Opéra was invited to give a series of performances in Washington. Sir Georg was conducting Mozart's *Le Nozze di Figaro* and in the middle of the performance accidentally stabbed his forehead with his baton. Blood began to spurt profusely and he quickly tried to stop this with his handkerchief. Luckily he had just reached a part of the work where there is a long section of recitative, in which the singers on stage are accompanied only by a harpsichord. He therefore quickly ran out of the pit (to the immense consternation of singers and orchestra alike) to get assistance. The stagehands quickly gave him some padding and cleaned the wound; Sir Georg ran back in and was able to pick up the baton and start conducting in time for the next piece which required the orchestra to play. It was only in the interval, when the house doctor was able to put a clean dressing on the wound, that he learned to his consternation what a lucky escape he had had – the doctor told him that he had missed a main artery on his head by less than a quarter of an inch.

Sir Georg Solti

In the sixties I was playing small parts (very small) and walking on, carrying spears, etc, at the National Theatre, where I was appearing in the Laurence Olivier *Othello*. I was in the dressing room playing Scrabble when the stage manager's voice came over the Tannoy system, *whispering*, 'Chris Timothy – you're off.' Like a bat out of hell I grabbed my wig and careered down several flights of stairs to the stage of the Old Vic. The scene was the famous carousing scene when Cassio is 'demoted'. I was one of a crowd singing and fighting in a drunken brawl. I got into the wings, grabbed the one remaining goblet off the 'props table' and, making loud 'I'm extremely drunk' noises, began staggering on to the lit stage – to find that that scene was over and the only people on the stage, in a very quiet, intimate scene, were Laurence Olivier (Othello) and Maggie Smith (Desdemona).

I was at least half-way across the stage before I realized! I was totally panic-struck! And instead of carrying on, I gasped in horror, went completely mute, and *backed* off the stage! Laurence Olivier, probably the greatest actor in the world, and my 'boss' at that time! If that isn't an embarrassing moment, tell me what is!

CHRISTOPHER TIMOTHY

It was New Year's Eve, many years ago. You can tell it was many years ago because I was driving through the snow from Finsbury Park to Braintree in Essex, after doing two shows in pantomime, in order to earn an extra £50 in cabaret. Among my props was a revolver, used in the act. I wasn't feeling funny. Heard my introduction, waited for the curtains to open, and they didn't. The band had (wisely) gone for a drink, so the silence was total. I fired the revolver and burst through the tabs.

Laughs? You could have heard a pin drop. The entire audience was gazing open-mouthed at three bullet holes banged in their very new, very very expensive velvet drapes.

TERRY SCOTT

Alongside at Dartmouth. In a rubber dinghy. Advising the children to get into the boat carefully. A large crowd watching. I am laden with bags and newspapers. I forget my own advice and step into fifteen feet of water and drop from sight. I surface, glasses intact on my nose and magazines under my arm, to a storm of wisecracks from the gathering crowd ('You'd better stick to TV', etc), and the children mockingly remind me of my lesson to them!

JONATHAN DIMBLEBY

(Excerpt from *Boat Crazy* by Graham Jones, published by Arrow Books)

PERSONAL APPEARANCE . . .

TOYAH WILLCOX

UNA STUBBS

MARJORIE PROOPS

LINDA LUSARDI

MAUREEN LIPMAN

MARTIN DANIELS

PAUL EDDINGTON

BARBARA DICKSON

MIKE YARWOOD

LES DAWSON

The only embarrassing moment I can remember is once in 1978. I was auditioning for a film called *The Corn is Green*, to be directed by George Cukor, starring Katharine Hepburn.

I had bright red hair at the time and when I walked into the room, George Cukor asked me if I would like to take my hat off. Of course I had to explain 'punk' to him. Miss Hepburn and he became very fond of my hair.

Toyah Willcox

I was shopping in Walton Street. I went into a very glamorous shop and started looking through the clothes. The assistant called, 'Can I help you?' I replied, 'May I please look?' to which she shouted, 'Madam, we are a dry cleaners, you know!'

Una Stubbs

Several years ago I was waiting in the queue to be checked by Customs at Calais. Standing behind me was a small group – of four or five – of nuns. I took a small step forward and down fell my knickers with a swoosh. In a split second those nuns had formed an encircling screen around me and, protected by their long black skirts, I was able to step out of my knickers and shove them in my handbag. Because of those nuns it was not nearly so embarrassing a moment as it might have been.

Marjorie Proops

On a modelling assignment in Oxford Street, I was asked to model a tiny nightie whilst standing on the step of a

61

London bus. The bus drove off without me and I had to walk back down Oxford Street wearing little else but a smile!!

LINDA LUSARDI

Some time ago I went to meet Julia McKenzie, a good friend of mine who was appearing in the musical *Follies*. We were going to discuss our mutual careers over a pot of tea in between the matinée and the evening show, as we were both at rather a crossroads.

I drove into town wearing a pair of large felt reindeer antlers, which I'd been given for Christmas and with which I hoped to raise a smile in Julia and Millie Martin's dressing room. I did indeed raise several smiles. We went to tea. I went back to the dressing room and picked up my things and returned to the car. I'd left the lights on and the battery had gone flat. I then spent about forty-five minutes stopping various cars and going to different garages and asking people if they had any jump leads – but nobody would help. So I returned to Julia's dressing room, and it was only when I looked in the mirror that I realized I was still wearing a pair of extremely large reindeer antlers. So there are several car drivers in London who have an even funnier view of Maureen Lipman than British Telecom have.

MAUREEN LIPMAN

In the summer of 1981 I was on stage in Newquay, performing a trick to a full house. During the performance I dropped a sponge ball; when I bent down to pick it up, there was a very loud ripping noise and yes, you've guessed it, there was a very large split in my trousers.

62

The audience roared with laughter, so rather than trying to cover up, I showed them all what I'd done, which made them fall about even more.

MARTIN DANIELS

I remember a moment of panic a few years ago when I was in a play called *Middle-Aged Spread* with Richard Briers.

I had to go on to the stage in a blackout, sit down at the dinner table and be revealed when the lights went up – eating yoghurt.

I dropped the spoon in the dark, bent down to retrieve it and was unable to rise again! My coat had caught under the chair leg. I thought I would have to play the scene lying down!

PAUL EDDINGTON

I was playing at the Usher Hall in Edinburgh in 1978 wearing a fruity batwing top, tight pants and high, high heels. I walked backwards at the end of a song into the darkness, but just as the light faded to black, I came up against a wedge-shaped sound monitor in the gloom and fell backwards, because I had folded at the knees: I sank, very ladylike, into a position rather like a stranded lady-bird! Two of the band came to my rescue as my pants were too tight for me to move! The worst thing of all was my mum was in the audience. I heard her groan as I went down into the sunset! Unfortunately I sparkled to the last, as my shoes had a row of *diamanté* down the high heels.

BARBARA DICKSON

Several years ago I bought two pairs of shoes which were identical except for the colour. One pair was black, and the other brown. I was appearing in Summer Season at the time and had just finished my act. As I went forward to take a bow I saw with horror that I had been on stage for almost an hour with one black shoe and one brown shoe!

MIKE YARWOOD

Once in a pantomime I went on stage dressed as the dame and was delighted by the gales of laughter I received every time I bent down. Then the stage manager pointed out – I'd forgotten to put on my knickers.

LES DAWSON

WHAT THE EYE DOESN'T SEE . . .

DAVID BLUNKETT

CHARLIE CHESTER

MARTIN DANIELS

When I was about to leave school I made one of those *faux pas* which remain with you forever. The Royal National Institute for the Blind had sent to my school one of its employment officers, who had come to talk to us about how to approach getting a job.

He was known as a rather well-meaning, but somewhat antiquated figure, who insisted that all those who went along to see a potential employer had to call him 'Sir', and doff their caps if they had them! It seemed to us at the time that he had quite a good job, and that we knew it all!

On this particular day I stalked out to where many of my fellow students were standing talking in the coffee break. 'Old Jennings is here,' I said. 'Come to keep himself in work.' To my horror a voice behind me said, 'That's right, lad, but I'm unlikely to last long trying to get you one!'

Always a hazard for blind people, not to know who is there when you make the all-revealing remark!

DAVID BLUNKETT

During the Korean War I went with a party of CSE (Combined Services Entertainments) to do shows all over Korea for our servicemen.

Apart from being a well-known comedian, I was also a writer for the *Sunday Dispatch*, and as well as entertaining the lads, I was a sort of war correspondent.

One of my principal jobs was to visit all the orphanages I could and report on them. At the time, there were thought to be about ten million displaced persons, of whom about two million were orphans.

On arrival at Pusan I was invited to the American Orphanage. When I arrived I saw a huge notice outside: HELL'S GARDEN : AMERICAN ORPHANAGE. I can't tell you the joy I experienced when I saw what these Americans were doing for those luckless kiddies; they were superb.

My next stop was the British Orphanage, and this was where I made the biggest *faux pas* of my life.

The notice outside the orphanage read: ILSIN ORPHANAGE AND RUBBISH DUMP! I was immediately incensed and complained to the major, saying that they may only be Korean orphans but I didn't think they should be listed with the rubbish. I really did go overboard with some of my comments.

However, the major let me go on and when I had finished he said quietly, 'Well, you see, we get no support or money for this, we do this completely off our own bat.' And then he explained, 'You see, if we put planks of wood, loaves of bread and tins of corned beef over there, and people take it, that would be stealing – *but if it's a rubbish dump . . .*'

The cleverness and the humanity of the British army made me blush with shame at what I had said.

It was a *faux pas* I still remember with pride.

CHARLIE CHESTER

Christmas 1987-8, I was in pantomime in Lewisham. I had a scene with Dave Lee Travis, who was playing the part of King Rat. In our scene Dave had to try and put me into a trance by hypnotizing me. Now Dave had been boasting to everyone before the panto that nobody could make him 'corpse' (laugh and forget his lines) but what he didn't know was that before the show my manager had written an extremely rude word on my eyelids. Consequently when I shut my eyes, Dave could read what had been written. He immediately collapsed on stage in a fit of laughter, unable to continue with what was supposed to be a fairly serious scene. The audience was in hysterics, and poor old Dave couldn't even tell them what had happened.

MARTIN DANIELS

A CASE OF MISTAKEN
IDENTITY . . .

Mark Wynter

Julie Walters

Sylvia Syms

Marcel Marceau

Bruce Kent

Glenda Jackson

Sir Christopher Foxley-Norris

Garret FitzGerald

John Fashanu

Roger de Courcey

Chas & Dave

Stirling Moss

Pam Ayres

Isla St Clair

Norman Collier

Jilly Cooper

Charlie Williams

I once congratulated an important television producer's wife on her expected arrival. She half nodded and turned away to speak with a friend. They both looked me up and down and moved on. A fellow actor whispered to me, 'You won't work here again!' It seemed the lady concerned had simply let herself go, and was deeply self-conscious about it. She was desperately trying to lose weight as she believed her husband had taken a slim trim mistress. My colleague was right, I have not worked at Elstree since!

MARK WYNTER

I once said to a woman at a party what an old bore a certain playwright was, only to discover I was speaking to his wife!

JULIE WALTERS

At the end of a performance of a play I was touring some years ago, I thanked the audience for their wonderful reception, saying, 'The Bath audiences are always so warm and it's a joy to play to them.' Unfortunately that week we were playing in Bournemouth.

SYLVIA SYMS

I met Arthur Miller, the playwright, and also Henry Miller, the American writer, and as I was a friend of both great men, I made a *faux pas*. One day, leaving Henry, I said to him, 'And now bye-bye, my dear Arthur . . .'

Of course he was not pleased – but there was nothing I could do about it.

MARCEL MARCEAU

I was about fifteen years old and my parents were having a party. A taxi came to the door at the end of the party and the driver said he had come for Mrs X. I asked around the room to find out who Mrs X was and a rather elderly lady was pointed out to me.

She was talking to a much younger man whose name apparently was also X. So I bowled up to them both and said to the man, 'Your mother's taxi is here.' He looked at me with a look that could kill and said, 'Not my mother, my wife.' I remember blushing through to my underwear. Nowadays I have got a rather thicker skin.

BRUCE KENT

I was at a Golden Globe dinner in Los Angeles, being introduced to the chairman. Smiling charmingly at the beautiful blonde beside him, I said, 'And is this your daughter?' to which he replied, 'No. This is my wife.' I wished that a hole in the floor would open for me to drop in.

GLENDA JACKSON

One day a few years ago, while I was Chairman of the Leonard Cheshire Foundation, I was in a lift on the ground floor of a building in the City of London. The doors of the lift were closing when I noticed a tall, distinguished-looking gentleman hurrying towards it. I put my foot in the doors, which duly opened for him. He was profuse in his thanks.

As we ascended together I looked at him more closely, and asked, 'Surely we've met before, haven't we?'

'Not since I gave you and your Trustees lunch last week,' he replied, to my acute embarrassment. Worse still, he turned out to be the Chairman of the Big Five Bank where our Foundation holds its main account.

Fortunately he was very much amused about it (he said).

SIR CHRISTOPHER FOXLEY-NORRIS

In 1975, when I was Minister for Foreign Affairs, I accompanied President O'Dalaigh on a state visit to France. Before dinner the 'top-table' guests were gathered in a drawing-room at the Elysée waiting for the guests to assemble in the dining-room. While all the others were engaged in animated conversation a man, whom I could not identify, and myself were standing silently at the back of the room. Feeling that I had to make conversation, I cast around desperately for some topic to broach. A recent newspaper article about the French president came into my mind and I said – humorously as I thought – to the man beside me, 'I read with interest recently of the president's decision to abolish all titles for guests in the Elysée save for the Comte de Paris and Prince Napoleon – the two pretenders to the French throne.' My companion made no response except a discouraging grunt and conversation lapsed. A few minutes later at table I asked Madame Giscard d'Estaing who this man was – he was seated quite near us. 'Prince Poniatowski, Minister of the Interior,' she replied. I now understood why my comment had not been so well received by my companion before dinner, but there was no way of putting it right as it would only have made matters worse to go up to him after dinner and tell him that I had not known who he was!

GARRET FITZGERALD

I gave a lift to a hitch hiker some time ago who spent the entire journey telling me what a close personal friend he was of John Fashanu and what a 'good bloke' he was. I waited until I dropped him off before introducing myself!

JOHN FASHANU

In 1966 as a Blue Coat at Pontins in Selsey, I met a family whose relative was Johnny Worth, the head man on the record side of Pye records. They said if I made a tape – I was singing then – they'd talk to Johnny Worth and tell him to look out for the tapes.

At that time while I was working under my real name of Roger Cooke, there was a famous duo called 'David and Jonathan' (handled by Johnny Worth at Pye). Their real names were Roger Cooke and Roger Greenway.

The plot thickens!

I phoned Pye a few weeks later.

'Can I speak to Johnny Worth?'

'Who's calling?'

'Roger Cooke!'

'Of course, I'll put you through.'

JW: 'Hello.'

RC: 'It's Roger Cooke here, John.'

JW: 'Hello, Roger – how's it going?'

RC: 'Fine – did you get the tape?'

JW: 'Where are you?'

RC: 'I'm working at Pontins.'

JW: 'Eh?'

RC: 'I'm a Blue Coat.'

JW: 'You're pulling my leg! What the hell are you doing there?'

Pause!

JW: 'Which Roger Cooke are you?'

RC: 'I'm the one who met your relatives' – (STOP!)

JW: 'Oh yes – I've got the tape – we'll let you know' – (CLICK)

ROGER DE COURCEY

In our early days, back in about 1973, long-time musicians Chas & Dave had begun writing songs. It was new! We'd never done it before! We were now song-writers! As soon as we'd finished a song we'd rush to the publisher. He'd draw up a contract, we'd sign, and rush back home with a copy to write another one. The contract sort of made 'em *real* songs! Not just something we'd 'made up'.

It was on one such visit that Dave made one of his famous *faux pas*!

Now Dave is one of the friendliest people you could wish to meet. He *always* makes a point of remembering your first name when he meets you. I sometimes forget and have to ask a second time, but Dave doesn't. He's proud of the fact, and rightly so. If I forget a name I ask Dave. He will argue black and blue if I disagree and he's always right. He knows it too! But there was one occasion, he says, when he wished he'd have taken more notice of me!

We'd gone to the publisher with a new song.

'Go down to my office,' says the publisher. 'You'll meet my new secretary, Godzilla, she's got a contract ready for you to sign!'

I smiled, picturing her, but didn't think any more of it. But Dave, unbeknown to me, had never heard of 'Godzilla'!

As we walked into the office, there was this girl. A bit unkind to refer to her as 'Godzilla', I thought, but she was on the *big* side.

Dave was in front of me. He's always in front when we meet new people, as if to say, 'I can handle this! I know who *this* is!'

'Pleased to meet you! I'm Dave! You're Godzilla, aren't you?'

I couldn't believe my ears! I crept round behind her, pretending to check out the publishers' tape machine or something, but turning and shaking my head like mad at Dave when I knew she couldn't see me!

But Dave was away! Charlie don't know, he's thinking. He never knows people's first names straight off like *I* do!

'Well, Godzilla, it's nice to have you working with us!'

I was making arm movements, head movements, eye movements, but it only seemed to make Dave more determined!

'You've got a contract for us to sign, Godzilla, haven't you?'

I'd given up.

'My name is *not* Godzilla!' said the poor girl at last.

The look on her face told Dave she wasn't pleased.

The look on Dave's face told me he had a nagging feeling that it wasn't just a simple case of getting a name wrong!

I can't remember how it ended up but it was friendly!

Dave said later, 'Well, *I've* never heard of Godzilla. I thought it was one of them Spanish tarts' names!'

It could have been 'King Kong'! It would have made no difference to Dave!

CHAS & DAVE

I was asked to appear in a celebrity charity event at Olympia, along with gold medallist showjumper David Broome. We were delighted to win the event.

A year later I bumped into Danny Blanchflower (whom I know) at a cocktail party.

'How are you?' I asked Danny.

'Fine!' said Danny. 'I have just returned from Ireland where I went to buy a horse.'

'What kind of a horse?' I enquired.

'A showjumper,' replied Danny.

'Aren't they rather expensive?' I said, looking a little confused – wondering what a footballer might do with a showjumping horse.

At that moment (fortunately for me) a small boy came over to us and asked:

'May I have your autograph, Mr Broome?'

STIRLING MOSS

I had gone into a fish and chip shop in Bude, Cornwall. While I was standing in the queue the man behind the counter kept looking at me. When I came to the front he said, 'You don't half look like Pam Ayres' and I said, 'I *am* Pam Ayres. That's why it is.' He looked at me in amazement, picked up a piece of fish and chip paper and asked me if I would sign it for his brother. I did. When I gave it back to him he kept on looking at it and saying things like, 'He'll never believe it! Not Pam Ayres! Not Pam Ayres!' So in the end I said, 'Why not? Why won't he believe it?' and the man said, 'Well, of all people, he can't stand you!'

PAM AYRES

I once asked Barry Sheene on a live TV show (*The Saturday Show*) if he missed his home, Australia, very much.

ISLA ST CLAIR

A lady wrote to me asking me to open a garden fête.

After spending two hours signing autographs and doing all the funnies, I was about to leave when she came up to me and said, 'Thank you for coming, Mr Daniels.' With that I pulled a handkerchief out of my pocket, pretending to do tricks; then she said 'Oh, you are clever!'

NORMAN COLLIER

I was signing books in London once, and after a two-hour session I went upstairs for a drink with the manager. There was a huge bunch of flowers in cellophane on the table.

'Oh, how lovely,' I screamed. 'Thank you so much.'

'They're for my wife,' said the manager hastily, and snatched them away.

JILLY COOPER

In the early 60's during my entertaining in the working mens clubs, I was stopped at the door of a club in Bradford and told it was a private club and could not go in. I said, 'Well who's going to pay me?'

He said, 'Why?' And I said, 'because I'm booked to appear here.'

He said, 'In that case old flower you'd better come in!!'

CHARLIE WILLIAMS

A DAY IN POLITICS . . .

Edwina Currie

Tony Benn

David Steel

Denis Healey

Paddy Ashdown

Tony Adams

Norman Tebbitt

My first job in politics was in Birmingham, where I was appointed Chairman of the Social Services Committee with a budget of around £50 million. I had been the youngest councillor and was the youngest chairman by a long way.

Soon after my appointment I travelled to London by train with the Director of Social Services, Ron Liddiard. We settled into our first class compartment and started doing some work.

The train stopped at Coventry and Tom White, the Director of Social Services for Coventry, got in.

'Morning, Ron.'

'Morning, Tom.'

'Who's this, your new secretary?'

'No, Tom, she's the boss!'

EDWINA CURRIE

On one occasion, speaking in Taunton at the by-election in 1956 or thereabouts, the chairman at the election meeting introduced the candidate as the man 'with whom on Thursday we shall strike a decisive blow *at* Great Britain'. He must have meant '*for* Great Britain', but the audience, being very well behaved and polite, cheered just as vigorously.

It was at the same meeting that one of the other speakers decided to launch into an attack on the then Prime Minister, Sir Anthony Eden, and his speech went like this:

'Sir Anthony Eden has been to Washington to see President Eisenhower. They issued a communiqué. He didn't have to go to Washington to issue that communiqué. Anybody could have written it. Tony Benn could have written it. It was *full* of clichés.'

The crowd cheered wildly, just as they had done earlier when, by mistake, and muddling me with the Prime Minister, he introduced me as Sir Anthony Benn.

TONY BENN

During the days of the Lib-Lab pact, I naturally had many meetings with the Prime Minister, Jim Callaghan. On one occasion I drove with my two assistants to Number 10 feeling very statesmanlike.

Such feelings were quickly dispelled, however, when on my way out, one of my assistants told me that the car would not start. I know that politicians are meant to cling to Number 10 when there, but I must be the only one who had to be physically pushed out of Downing Street.

DAVID STEEL

I think the best *faux pas* I can currently think of is that when I went to the USA, President Reagan greeted me in the White House with 'How nice to see you again, Mr Ambassador!'

DENIS HEALEY

My most embarrassing moment was one day when I visited somebody who had asked me to come and see them about repairs to their council house. I had been on six previous calls before I reached them late in the evening. At each of the previous calls I had been given a cup of coffee. The result was that I was, to use the vernacular, 'cross-legged'.

As luck would have it my constituent's problem was the basin in his bathroom. This was hanging off the wall, but the tap still worked. He proved this by running the water, which only made my predicament worse.

In the corner of the bathroom I saw precisely what I was looking for, a WC. I asked him if I could use it.

It may have been the sheer relief, but I pulled the chain on the cistern with more than my customary vigour and the whole lot came crashing to the floor. Coming back in my constituent asked me, in what I thought was rather a tart voice, whether I expected him still to vote Liberal after this.

It was a deeply embarrassing moment, but has now become rather a funny one. As it happened my constituent did vote Liberal and now frequently sees me in the town, never losing an opportunity, of course, to pull my leg!

PADDY ASHDOWN

Many years ago I was coming back from the Isle of Wight after a sailing weekend, and as I arrived on Southampton station the London train was pulling out. British Rail had a special arrangement with the Isle of Wight ferry and that was to miss it!! I spoke to a porter who informed me that the train was full but another one was behind. It was a non-corridor, non-stopping train to London. I was dying to spend a penny so I dived into the loo. The thought of 'non-corridor' was too much for my bladder! When I came out the train was about to leave so I jumped into the nearest compartment somewhat out of breath.

Sitting alone was a middle-aged man in a light grey suit, blue shirt and tie. 'I know you,' I thought, but being somewhat shy I either sit there uncomfortably, perspiring, hating myself for *not* saying anything, or I go the other way – this time it was the latter!

'Hello,' I said. I got a stern look. 'How are you?' I got another stern look. 'Where have we worked together?' Was it *Crossroads*, I thought, is it John Bently? Perhaps it was in panto? The awful silence was to become the overture to more sweating and an embarrassing journey as I realized my companion was Edward Heath!!!

TONY ADAMS

I am always in some difficulty when asked this sort of question. My only really awful faux pas was to tell anyone about my other faux pas, so I never do it anymore!

NORMAN TEBBITT

THE OPPOSITE SEX...

Julia Somerville

Rik Mayall

David Jacobs

Leslie Crowther

Norman Collier

When I was presenting the nine o'clock news one night I didn't realize that my microphone was still turned up. My voice was clearly heard over some shots of a group of men leaving some top-level talks, saying, 'Who's that gorgeous bloke in the background?' I had difficulty hiding my blushes when they came back to me! And by the way, I never did find out who he was.

JULIA SOMERVILLE

When I was at Manchester University I was in love with a girl who worked in my local chip shop. Completely besotted. So much so that I could hardly go into the shop in case she looked at me and I blushed and had to run away. Having done that, I'd never be able to return and I'd never see her again.

Anyway, one day I was very hungry, there was nothing in the house and I had to brace the chip shop.

I looked in the window. There was no one behind the counter. Whoever was serving was in the back room. I went in. I was alone in the shop. Then *she* appeared. Utterly brain-mincingly gorgeous and radiant. I felt I was soiling her beauty merely by my presence. *I had to be cool.* I was going to have chicken pie and chips but *I had to be cool.*

'Yes,' she breathed.

'Er, chicken and chips please,' I heard myself saying. Surely that was the coolest thing they sold.

'Leg or breast,' said the goddess.

Our eyes met for the last time as I said, 'What are your breasts like?'

For a full five seconds we looked into each other's eyes as I went from pink to red to purple and all my insides decided they had become semolina. Then I ran away. Never to return.

And if you read this, chip lady, *I still love you.*

RIK MAYALL

It was a fairly cold autumn evening in south-east London; I was introducing a beauty competition in one of the few remaining large surburban cinemas. Rather like the weather, the girls were, to say the least, fairly dreary, but no matter: I was not a judge, merely the compére. Backwards and forwards trooped the nervous young ladies, to the whistles and shouts of their friends and families who made up the audience of about fifty people in the 2500-seater picture palace.

When it came to the exciting last moments I announced the first three in the time-honoured fashion of reverse order. The girl who came third got a few boos and a couple of wolf-whistles, the girl who came second received much the same. And then the moment they'd all been waiting for – I announced the winner and gave her number. This was greeted with more boos than usual, and when I saw the girl come on I realized why. I had called out the wrong number! Instead of calling out number six I had the card upside-down and had called out number nine. There was nothing I could do except admit my terrible mistake, whereupon the girl burst into tears and stormed off the stage. By this time number six, the real winner, was practically fainting in the wings because she was the hot favourite and hadn't until then even made the first three.

My embarrassment was such that to placate the poor sobbing loser I presented her with an equivalent first prize out of my own pocket. Thank goodness it was an affordable 9-inch television set and not a Concorde trip to New York.

DAVID JACOBS

Like most little boys, I developed the usual healthy interest in the opposite sex. I spent hours wondering what they looked like without their clothes on. The fact that one could see little girls wandering about stark naked in local paddling pools, or by the seaside, was unimpressive. They were only toddlers, so they didn't count! It was one's contemporaries at school that one mentally stripped in the playground.

I had my first break at the age of eight, when a nubile young lady of the same age – or maybe she was a year or two older – virtually picked me up in the school holidays, and invited herself round for tea. My mother suggested that we should go upstairs and play in my bedroom after tea, a suggestion that Deirdre Bosworth seized upon eagerly. You see, I even remember her name! Once upstairs, she offered me a tour of inspection. Breathlessly I accepted her offer, and she divested herself of her blouse and vest. 'Those are called breasts,' she declared. I was not impressed. I'd seen fat boys in the showers who were bigger than she was!

This is probably why, when I was twelve and at a co-educational school in Twickenham, I evolved MY PLAN. Not only were the girls of my age infinitely shapelier by then, but we all used to go to the same public baths for swimming lessons. Our changing rooms were divided by a wooden screen which started at the ceiling but didn't quite reach the ground: the kind of gap that enterprising West Indians are said to limbo underneath and so get in free! I bought a pocket mirror and instructed my mates to do the same. At the next opportunity, we placed the mirrors in a row on the floor under the screen which divided us from the girls, and by skilfully tilting them we saw the lot!

The following week we were surprised to hear sounds of uncontrolled mirth coming from the other side of the screen. Staring aghast at the floor, we saw a row of mirrors tilted towards us. It wasn't their retaliation that rankled – it was their laughter! Mind you, it was a very cold day!

LESLIE CROWTHER

We were about to move house and I had been working away for a few days in Cabaret, I arrived home early hours of the morning. I let myself in the house with the front door key. My arms were full of things, I had a suit over one arm, and I was struggling in the dark. I went into the lounge and put my suit over where I thought the settee was when I heard a plop. I managed to put the light on and found my suit lying on the floor with no furniture in the house. My wife had moved without telling me. (Joke) She thought it was very funny. It was a good job I didn't get undressed to get into bed.

NORMAN COLLIER

ON THE BOX . . .

Tom O'Connor

Lulu

Michael Buerk

Robin Knox-Johnston

Jan Leeming

Dora Bryan

I think my biggest *faux pas* was when I compered *Name that Tune*, and started the show without the answers to the Golden Medley – seven tunes in thirty seconds.

Fortunately I happened to know six of them, and guessed the contestant was right with his seventh guess.

So he won £1000 never knowing the fear in my heart.

TOM O'CONNOR

When I appeared on the *Kilroy-Silk* programme once, I had so much to say for myself, and was so busy interrupting poor Mary Archer just as she was about to make a most cogent remark, when my mind went completely blank, right there in front of the cameras and about one million or so viewers! I was stunned into silence and could only laughingly apologize to everyone involved.

LULU

In early 1970 I was a guest on the *Frost Show* in New York. The guest who followed me was Dyan Cannon, the film actress, and as she came on to the stage she said to me that she admired the single-handed non-stop circumnavigation of the world that I had completed the previous year, and would love to make a voyage like that.

I replied that if she was interested she could join me on my next trip, and I added 'I don't guarantee that we'll make it, but it would be fun trying.'

The audience of six hundred went terribly quiet, whilst Dyan Cannon looked flustered and confused. I took a moment to realize that in America 'make it' has a totally different meaning to that which I had intended. Fortunately David Frost realized the embarrassment, and quickly changed the subject!

ROBIN KNOX-JOHNSTON

My most embarrassing moment in broadcasting was when I had a nose-bleed on the air. It was in a news programme in which a number of contributors were seated around a table. I had just started my report when my nose began to pour. I battled on manfully, spraying blood liberally over the others who scrambled to salvage their scripts from the deluge.

Luckily I was in radio at the time and the listeners remained ignorant of the bloody scenes behind the microphone.

MICHAEL BUERK

In the early sixties I was for a while a presentation announcer for ABC in Sydney (that's the Australian equivalent of the BBC). The presentation announcers used to come into vision in between programmes, either to introduce what was coming next, or to give a menu of the evening's events, or even to promote programmes appearing later in the week. We had fairly long shifts and I remember one occasion when I had been promoting a rather important current-affairs programme. The promotion had gone on for most of the day because they were interviewing the United States Under-Secretary of State for Far Eastern Affairs – said quickly this can be quite a mouthful.

The evening wore on and I got a little more tired, and my announcement about 'the United States Under-Secretary of State, etc, etc' came out as 'the United States *under-sexed* Secretary of State'. Was my face red!

JAN LEEMING

I was invited on to an afternoon chat show for Tyne Tees Television when I was appearing in the north-east. It was a charming studio set, with the usual chairs in strategic interviewing positions, and surrounded by a series of plants, in which the protea plant featured largely. It's always nice to have something original to say on chat shows, and I did know something about these particular plants, so I thought that would make a good gambit. The programme opened, and as I hadn't been briefed about the other guest, a very pleasant lady, who was sitting next to me, I thought I'd warm up proceedings. Chat shows can be sticky sometimes, especially if the inter-viewees are nervous, and slight nervousness always makes me chat more. 'You really ought to get these pro-tea plants out of here,' I said. 'They look nice, but they're terrible things really, you know.' The interviewer raised her eyebrows and politely and smilingly asked why.

'Ooh, well, they harbour beetles,' I announced sagely. 'I was once on board ship, coming back from South Africa. I'd been doing a revue out there, and the family was with me. When we sailed I was horrified to find a black beetle in my bed. The steward said it was from my farewell present of protea flowers. When the captain found out there were protea plants on board he ordered that they should all be thrown over the side.' I got into my stride, and rambled on about people feeling itchy, and the dreadful consequences of protea plants. Everyone continued to smile pleasantly, but there was a slight stiffening of the spine from the other interviewee, and I thought I detected a swift exchange of glances on set. It was not until the programme was over, and I was back in the hospitality room that it was explained to me that the protea plants decorating the studio that afternoon had all been provided by the other guest on the programme, who happened to be a representative of a horticultural firm. They were hoping to import the plants. I really was upset, and hoped I didn't damage their trade too much that afternoon. How I wished that someone had told me who the other guest was before the cameras started to roll.

DORA BRYAN

(Excerpt from *According to Dora*, by Dora Bryan, published by The Bodley Head)

102

NEVER WORK WITH ANIMALS OR CHILDREN . . .

Dr Benjamin Spock

Jimmy Cricket

Frank Carson

Norman Collier

A mother came into the emergency room of Presbyterian Hospital with her baby. The baby was perhaps eight months of age. She said that the baby had swallowed the safety pin from the diaper. While she had been changing the baby, she had taken out the pin, laid it down and got out a fresh diaper. She had looked for the pin and it wasn't there. So she *knew* the baby had swallowed it. She was hysterical and crying. I tried to reassure her because obviously the baby was quite comfortable.

I suggest that we fluoroscope the baby. We went into the fluoroscope room, laid the baby down on the table, turned off the light, and turned on the fluoroscope. I brought the screen down over the baby's head. 'See, there's the skull, there's the mouth, there's the throat, and there's the chest.' We didn't see any safety pin. As we got to the lower abdomen, into view came a huge safety pin. It looked as big as one used on a horse blanket, because it was distorted and enlarged by its relationship to the fluoroscope screen.

The mother screamed and fainted dead away on the floor. While I was reviving her, I discovered that the safety pin we saw was the safety pin still in the baby's diaper. The mother had got another pin to use on the diaper before bringing the baby to the hospital. I hadn't taken off the baby's diaper and it was this pin that showed up on the fluoroscope. I tried to explain this to the mother, but she was utterly unconvinced. She thought I was just giving her sweet talk. She was even more convinced that the baby had swallowed the safety pin than before.

DR BENJAMIN SPOCK

Once when I was performing in a very small working-men's club in the north of England a very large bumble bee kept flying round the stage in the middle of my act. I kept chasing it and needless to say it went down well with the audience. When I had finished my act I opened up a matchbox and said, 'Come on, boy, it's time for the next club,' pretending I took it with me everywhere.

JIMMY CRICKET

My next-door neighbour's cat was held firmly in the jaws of my bulldog. I couldn't open his jaws and rang the vet. He couldn't come, so I drove like mad to his surgery, and got a speeding ticket that earned me an endorsement plus a fine of £80.

The vet gave the dog an injection and he went to sleep, his jaws relaxed and we freed the cat who was dead. I then went back to my next-door neighbour and apologized for the bulldog's behaviour. My neighbour laughed and said the cat had died of a heart attack and he had buried it in his back garden. The bulldog had dug it up.

FRANK CARSON

I had an embarrassing time when I did a Summer Season in Great Yarmouth. Accommodation was hard to get and I had to take a caravan on a caravan site. One day I went to the loo and there were a few children playing around outside. Suddenly a voice shouted, 'Can we have your autograph?' and a piece of paper was pushed under the toilet door for me to sign. I thought the paper was for something else.

NORMAN COLLIER

SPORTING GESTURES . . .

Fatima Whitbread

Roy Walker

The Beverley Sisters

Tessa Sanderson

Joe Johnson

Bryan Gunn

Lucinda Green

Duncan Goodhew

Mike Gatting

Geoff Capes

Bill Beaumont

At Gateshead last year on 13 June at the Kodak Classic meeting, my team colleague sprayed some 'freezer' on my back, which was hurting me. Unfortunately I pulled my shorts down too far, and the next day's press showed pictures of the incident with a prominent proportion of my bottom in full view! The captions used by the press alongside the pictures were also a source of amusement to many people.

FATIMA WHITBREAD

I had the pleasure of being invited to the Four Stars Golf Tournament 1987. I appeared at Grosvenor House on the Tuesday in the cabaret, along with such great stars as Jimmy Tarbuck, Ronnie Corbett, Des O'Connor; and sitting in the audience were big stars like Joan Collins, Telly Savalas, Victor Mature and, of course, Her Royal Highness Princess Anne.

I had a terrific night, it really went down well and I was looking forward to golf at the famous Moor Park Golf Club.

The first day it rained constantly. The second day the sun shone so I decided to turn out in matching yellow clothes. I played a round for about six holes and as we came close to the clubhouse, that beautiful historic club-house, lots of celebrities came out to watch us play.

I had played a good shot right down the fairway. I was just about to play my second shot to the green when I noticed a piece of straw sticking out from behind the ball. I bent down to pull it away from the ball and I heard the most tremendous rip I've ever heard in all my life. I knew immediately what it was: my trousers had burst – not just a little but the full length of the seam. I was red with embarrassment. I heard the crowd laugh and I turned round. Who was laughing the most? None other than Joan Collins! By now I'd turned scarlet. My caddy quickly relieved the embarrassing situation by giving me my waterproof trousers which I hurriedly pulled on, and I beat a hasty retreat down the fairway. I don't think I hit a golf ball properly for the rest of the week. Yes, I shall never forget the Four Stars Golf Tournament.

ROY WALKER

Our marvellous Dad would occasionally take an excited Joy to football matches when she was a child. So Joy was no stranger to football when in 1958 she married Billy Wright, the England Football Captain.

The media loved the romance of England's lovely young TV star and its soccer hero with his record number of caps for his country. The press turned out in full whenever they appeared together.

Teddie and I were taken to see him play on the grand occasion of a World Cup game and we joined Joy in the Directors' box at Wembley. The game was explained to us, and fans stopped looking at the Beverley Sisters as the game got under way.

All went well during the first half, with excited spectators rising as one body when the English team was successful. Champagne (tea for Teddie and I) was served at the interval and then it was back to the Director's box when the game resumed. Suddenly Teddie and I leapt to our feet with great excitement, clapping, cheering and shouting goal! We were amazed and embarrassed in the silence that surrounded us to find ourselves the *only* ones on our feet.

Nobody had explained to us that the sides change ends at half-time, so that the goal-mouth they had been aiming at in the first half became the opponents' goal-mouth in the second half, and England then had to shoot the other way.

So it appeared to all the other 'bigwigs' in the box, and the fervent football fans near us at Wembley that day, that the Beverley twins were overjoyed that the opposition had scored the *only* goal of the match!

THE BEVERLEY SISTERS

Here is a funny thing that happened to me in 1984 when I went to Hungary to train.

Three days after we arrived in Hungary, we decided to have our first training throwing session. When I was asked to get ready, I went to put on my javelin boots and, oh my God, guess what – I had brought two right feet out with me.

Of course, my colleagues rolled over laughing when they saw this because running down the runway my feet looked as though they were travelling the wrong way, away from me. I am glad to say that I remembered the right foot and the left foot for the Olympics in Los Angeles and happy to say that it brought me lots of luck.

TESSA SANDERSON

In 1978 I was invited to take part in a snooker invitation tournament at Grimsby. The other players included Steve Davis, Tony Meo, Jimmy White and Willy Thorne. I set off from home, allowing myself plenty of time to get to Grimsby, and arrived an hour before the scheduled starting time. I walked into the snooker club and was confronted by a man who said, 'You're not playing tonight, Joe.' I said, 'Yes I am,' and it was then I discovered that I was an hour early but a week late; the competition had been the previous week. Needless to say I packed my cue and went home rather embarrassed.

JOE JOHNSON

My worst experience in football came in Mexico in 1983. We were playing in the Youth World Cup for Scotland against teams like South Korea, Australia and Mexico. In the games against South Korea and Australia we played in a place called Toluca. This place was poverty stricken and there were some awful sights. In one of the games I felt something hit me in the back as I was standing in the goal. I looked round and was shocked to see a plastic bag on the ground. I picked this up and in the bag were rotten fish heads and eyes: it was not a very nice sight. I was nearly sick. We went on to win the game so I was not too bothered afterwards.

BRYAN GUNN

There was a large crowd around the prize-giving table at the 1987 Tetbury Horse Trials, boosted by the presence of Princess Anne. I was busy talking to someone on the outside edge of this crowd. The prize giving started and various class winners were duly presented. Suddenly someone nudged me and said, 'It's you now, they're doing the advanced class.' Not wanting to keep anyone waiting, I burst through the crowd as quickly as I could, walked up to the table, grasped the sponsor by the hand and took the red ribbon that was in his other hand. There was a silence and he did not let go of the rosette. Then the microphone spoke, 'But Lucinda, you haven't won it, you were only second.'

LUCINDA GREEN

I had a very embarrassing moment; I was swimming and the cord to my swimsuit broke. It was terrible – I was swimming backstroke!

DUNCAN GOODHEW

I was on my first tour abroad with the full England side. In my very first match against a New Zealand team, I was called upon to bowl. At that time I bowled rather more regularly than I do now, so I was keen to make an early impression. I certainly did that. Everything went well until I was about to leap into my delivery stride, but then my foot slipped under me, I collapsed backwards and was left flat on my back still clutching the ball. The entire team doubled up with laughter and my England career had begun.

Also, at a Headingley Test match, one player hit a six which bounced harmlessly among the crowd and landed in front of the St John's Ambulance caravan, where it was picked up by one of their ladies. Unfortunately she failed to reach the pitch with her return throw and hit one of the spectators on the head.

MIKE GATTING

I had an embarrassing moment early on in my career when I was running the 200 metres in a pentathlon event. Unfortunately my jock-strap broke in front of two lady timekeepers who both subsequently neglected to record my time!

GEOFF CAPES

I was still playing rugby when I began appearing as a panellist in *A Question of Sport*. That was five years ago, and now there are young people watching the programme who don't know me as a former player; to them I am the guy who never gets his rugby questions right.

This horrible reputation took root when Willie Carson knew the answer to my rugby question and I didn't. If the ground could have opened up in front of me, I would gladly have jumped inside.

The producer enjoyed my embarrassment so much that, ever since, the researchers have been ferreting out the most obscure rugby questions for me and the most obscure soccer questions for Emlyn Hughes. Compared with the questions they throw at us, the guest panellists are let off lightly. Emlyn and I are the scapegoats – the men they love to see struggling.

One of my more long-drawn-out blunders had to do with the Russell Cargill Trophy. The what? The Russell Cargill Trophy. If you don't know, and I didn't, it's what your team get if they win the Middlesex Sevens. I was asked to name the current holders and, not knowing what the trophy was, failed to score.

Next year David Coleman said: 'Bill, you know what the Russell Cargill Trophy is?'

'Yes,' I said, all bright and smart, 'it's for the Middlesex Sevens. Wasps won it last year.'

'Yes,' said David, 'and who were runners-up?'

See, if I'd kept my mouth shut, he'd have asked me who won it. But I didn't. So he didn't. And I got it wrong. It caused a slight stir at the time. People in the street were saying: 'Hmm. Must be a bit of a dummer, that bloke. Doesn't know who were the runners-up for the Russell Cargill Trophy. Or anything else about rugby.'

BILL BEAUMONT

(Excerpt from *Bedside Rugby* by Bill Beaumont, published by William Collins (Willow Books), 1986)

ACKNOWLEDGEMENTS

The NSPCC would like to acknowledge with thanks permission to quote from the following books:

According to Dora by Dora Bryan by permission of The Bodley Head.

Bedside Rugby by Bill Beaumont by permission of William Collins.

Boat Crazy by Graham Jones by permission of Arrow Books.

Caught in the Act by Richard Todd by permission of Century Hutchinson.

The Eye of the Wind by Sir Peter Scott by permission of Hodder & Stoughton.

Politics Apart by Roy Hattersley by permission of BBC Enterprises Ltd.

Ramblings of An Actress by Sheila Hancock by permission of Hutchinson.

The Story of the Shadows by Mike Reed by permission of Hamish Hamilton.